Dark Night

A

Wilderness

Experience

I dedicate this book to my mother Rosie Hill; may she rest in peace. And to my children and grandchildren, Kyle, Gabrielle, Samuel, Faith, Alyssa, and Rashad Jr.

Chapter 1
Dark Night

Psalm 13; 16:7; 22:2; 25:16-19; 139:12, 23-24

The dark night of the soul is a term used long ago. I would describe it this way; the further you walk in the wilderness the darker it gets, until its pitch black. You are surrounded by complete blackness. It's in the dark night that you will experience brokenness, spiritual growth, and healing. God chooses when and for how long this will happen. Anywhere from a few months to a few years. For me, mines lasted 9 years. Anything that once had meaning and purpose will suddenly become meaningless. Nothing will make sense anymore, and you will begin to question everything that exists, even your belief in God.

The wilderness is a place of necessity. It may not seem like it while you're walking through it, but it is. It's a place of testing, transformation, and transition. This can happen one by one or all three at the same time. It's a very intense purging, which will be extremely overwhelming. Some people have committed suicide or walked away from God because they had no knowledge of what they were going through.

It's in the dark night that you realize you never really knew God, and everything you thought you knew was all man and not God.

It's in the darkest of the night where God turns you upside down and shakes everything out of you. And the only thing left is the dirt frame known as the body. It's in the night season all that is hidden shall come to light. God will show you the true content of your heart. You will be surprised and ashamed at what He shows you about, "YOU".

In the night season, God allows the enemy to use people and situations for what He needs to accomplish in you. There will be betrayed, unexplained sicknesses, and death (loved ones, dreams, prophecies, visions, plans, and ministries). One or all of these will occur. In my case, all of them happened. I suggest you read the Book of Job, and about Joseph.

You will experience every emotion that exists; hatred, bitterness, anger, fear, depression, grief, anxiety, love, etc. I suggest you read Lamentation 2:15-22, and Chapter 3.

At the end of the dark night, you come out broken, humbled, and filled with the love of God. People will no longer see you, they will see HIM. Read Deuteronomy 8:2-6.

*I pray this book will help bring clarity to anyone experiencing a deep intense stripping than the normal wilderness experience.

Chapter 2
Reason for the Dark Night

I've learned that there are different levels in the wilderness. But the most painful is the night season.

We have all been hurt at some point in our lives. Some worse than others. For those of us who didn't heal properly, it begins to manifest through our behavior. The enemy of your soul likes to wound you in childhood so that you become a dysfunctional adult. Later in life, there are more injuries added to the ones you already have.

Now, God calls you and saves you. There are things that instantly drops off, and there are things deep in your soul that lay dormant. For some of us, it's not until you start your ministry journey they start to appear. You start off happy and on fire, doing the work of the Lord. While deep in your soul festers all of life's issues you haven't dealt with. You must understand demons are assigned to you and they have followed you all of your life. They know your weaknesses and shortcomings. When God feels its time, He allows the enemy to create situations that will awake those things that are asleep.

We have a lot of wounded soldiers in leadership with gangrenous personalities. Spiritually killing people faster than cancer. Just like a flesh wound, if left untreated will become infected and will spread to the rest of your body. Depending on the type of infection it could kill you, like gangrene. That's what is happening in the body of Christ today. Now your walk with God is affected, and that is when He sends you into the wilderness.

There are many personalities. But there are some personalities developed from the trauma they experienced.

Example:
- rape/molestation – you tend to have trust and intimacy issues, suspicious in personal relationships, anger, etc.
- Abuse – Depression, low self-esteem, social isolation, poor self-image, suicidal thoughts, may become an abuser themselves, people pleaser mentality. Some get into abusive relationships thinking it's a form of love, etc.
- Infidelity – Controlling, resentment, trust issues, unforgiving, jealous, envious, low self-image, mood shifts, rage, self-protective, easily triggered, compulsive spending or eating, etc.

This is just a few of life's traumas and the traits that follow. Believe it or not, this can cause you to put God on the same level as man. The only way to get closer to God is to be purged of all of this. We all know that hurt people, hurt people. You walk in dysfunction until God says its time. Time for what? THE WILDERNESS!

Chapter 3
FAMILY SECRETS

1996, a beautiful Prophetess gave me a prophetic word that I would go through a shaking nothing as I've ever experienced before in my life, but it would be for my good. It would feel like the bottom of the earth was yanked from underneath me, and again, it was for my good. Afterward, God would use me in a mighty way. He was going to bless me with my heart's desires. Needless to say, this was one of those words you never want to hear. This word began in January 2008. It was the beginning of sorrows. Let me start by giving you a clear picture of why this had to take place.

I had a very unusual childhood. My family gave the meaning to the word, Dysfunctional. I'm a firm believer that, a person should talk their problems out instead of giving the delusion that life is perfect.

My father was a hardworking man, who enjoyed drinking beer after work to relax. The only problem with that was the fact that he couldn't control his anger when he drank. I grew up with my father beating my mother on a daily basis. My brother was 10 years old and I was 5, the only children my parents had. We called my brother Baby Huey because he was a big kid for his age. Whenever my father started to fight my mother I was the only one that helped her. My brother would go hide in a corner and urinate on himself. They were extremely jealous of one another. If a man looked at her or a woman looked at him, they would argue, and the arguments lead to fighting. One day my mother decided that she would try to scare him by shooting at his hand. She thought maybe this would scare him enough to make him stop. But the bullet ricocheted off the wall and went into his chest. Normally, if I had heard them fighting I would run into the room and jump on my father's back to try to stop him. But for some reason this time I didn't.

It was a warm Saturday morning. My brother and I were in his room watching television when we heard a loud, "BOOM". I looked at my brother and said, "I bet you it was daddy", he said, "no, I bet you it was mom". I heard my mother screaming, "Oh my God, oh my God". We ran towards the kitchen. I watched my father as he crawled into the kitchen and collapsed on the floor onto his back as he was spitting up blood, my mother was screaming and crying as she dialed 911. Not understanding what I was watching, I walked up to my father and stood over him. He looked into my eyes, and then slowly his eyes rolled into the back of his head. The first thought that came to my mind was that I won the bet. The second thought was the abuse was over and that my mommy could be happy. I didn't realize that I would never see him again. That trauma would set the course of a dysfunctional personality you wouldn't believe.

As I looked up, I noticed that my uncle and his best friend who was like an uncle, was standing behind me, everybody was in shock. It felt like everything went in slow motion. One of my uncles swept me up and rushed me to his apartment which was located in the basement of the building where we lived. I remember days passing by and I hadn't seen my mother. I was finally informed that she was in jail. Weeks later, we were on our way to the Court House. My uncle and my older cousin were coaching me on what to say to the Judge. Of course, I didn't remember any of it. One by one we went into the judge's chambers. When my turn came my older cousin went in with me. I told the judge

11

everything that I could remember. He looked at me and said, "Your story is the only story that I believe. Because of you, I'm going to let your mother go". A few days had gone by before my mother came home. That was the happiest day of my life.

We never received any counseling, nor did anybody ever bring it up. Except for me, I talked about it every chance I got. I would ask questions, but I would never get any answers. My family never talked about what had happened. My mother kept everything bottled up on the inside, nor did she forgive herself for what she had done. The family never sought counseling for my brother and me. They believed in sweeping secrets under the rug. I guess they thought it would disappear and everything would go back to normal.

The next 7 years my mother tried to make life as normal as possible for me and my brother, and she did. My mother bought a house in an all-white neighborhood. Life was wonderful at that time, so I thought. Whatever I wanted she made sure I got it. We had expensive clothes, furniture, cars, etc. You name it we had it. I went back to visit my old neighborhood where my uncles and cousins still lived. Over time my old friends and family let me know that I wasn't accepted anymore. They called me, "Oreo Cookie", black on the outside and white on the inside because I didn't speak incorrect English anymore. You would think calling me Oreo cookie would be harsh enough, but it wasn't.

I was the ugly duckling in the family. I wore very thick glasses and I had thick coarse hair. They went from saying my glasses were thick as a coke bottle, to calling them thick as a whole case. Saying I had low self-esteem would be an understatement. Then, suddenly back at home people started moving out of the neighborhood. I soon found out it was because of the black family that moved in. Now I had to deal with the fact that I wasn't black enough for the black people, and I was too black for the white people. I didn't fit in anywhere. As long as I had my mother I knew things would be alright, so I thought.

By the age of 12, I was so shy I could hardly function. I was in junior high, I was trying to adjust to the school change. My mother started to withdraw from people and started displaying strange behaviors. She began to think that we were trying to kill her because of what she had done to our father. My family, still in denial;

never did anything to help her until it was almost too late. My once peaceful home became a constant battlefield. One morning, as I was getting ready for school there was a knock at my front door. It was two of the most popular girls in the neighborhood. They informed me that my mother had jumped out of her upstairs bedroom window and the police were trying to find out where she lived. I thanked them, waited for the police and then I called my uncles.

They took her to the hospital, where she stayed for two weeks. She was diagnosed with having bipolar with psychosis. After my mother came home she was on so many different kinds of medications. Not liking how the meds made her feel, she stopped taking them and that's when my life as a child ended.

She started breaking my brother's belongings and attacking him for no reason. At that time, we didn't know anything about mental illness. We didn't understand what was happening. I began reading a psychology book, trying to understand what had happened to my once loveable mother. I don't remember the name of the book, but I read a paragraph on trauma; how it could cause a chemical imbalance, and how talking about your problems could relieve stress. Remember what I said earlier, she never talked about what happened.

Watching my mother go through this mental breakdown, my brother couldn't take it any longer. He left for the Army and never came home again. I later learned of the hatred he had for her. Till this day I haven't seen him in over 37 years. With me being the only person there at home, I instantly became the enemy; that's when the abuse started.

After my brother's departure, she turned her anger towards me. She hated me with such an unimaginable hatred, and it happened overnight. She told me she was going to kill me and believe me she tried. She said she wished that I had never been born and that the only thing I would be good for is sex. Wow, that's a self-esteem booster.

This kind of living became routine for me. With my mother being mentally ill she stopped paying the bills. One day we received a foreclosure letter. I called the bank and pleaded with the woman not to take our house. She asked, "Baby how old are you?", I told her 13. I explained what was going on, she asked if I had any family members that could help me, I told her no. I heard her sniffing and her voice cracking. Then she said, "I'm going to help you as much as I can", and she did. I was

15

a mess mentally. Love could have stood right in front of me, I wouldn't have recognized it. At this time, I was saved and, in the church, Church Of God In Christ. I thought with God on my side I was safe, my life would become better again.

They taught me man's traditions and how to shout, but no Word. The more I prayed the worse things became. I would gather my neighborhood friends together in my living room and teach them the little I knew about God. I really had a hunger for Him, just didn't have the right teachers.

One day during my prayer time, I was on my knees by the side of my bed. My mother stood in my doorway. Her voice changed, and she asked me, "Where's your God at now". I prayed harder, but nothing. Within seconds, she attacked me. After that, I left the church. I thought to myself, what's the use, God hates me too.

One early winter morning, I woke up to the doors off the hinges and all the faucets on full blast, with all the windows up. I got out of bed to put the windows down. She walked up behind me, spun me around and punched me in the nose. Blood began to pour out like a water fountain. I ran to the bathroom, which was the only door she hadn't taken off. I managed to lock myself inside until she tired herself out. Later that day I heard her go back upstairs to her room. I came out of the bathroom, put the doors back on the hinges, put my clothes on and left for the day. My neighbors became used to me running to their houses for safety; one neighbor had a first aid kit just for me. By the time I had started high school I didn't know whether I was coming or going, I just couldn't focus. I was too ashamed to say anything to anybody. Due to the abuse, I had missed so many days of school. One day in my nursing class, my teacher looked at me, and in front of the class said, "You are going to be a dropout, with dropout babies and on welfare". I felt like dying. Later, that same day in my Algebra class I kept raising my hand trying to answer a math question, but the teacher would never acknowledge me. One of the students brought to his attention that my hand was raised, he said in front of the class, "She will never amount to nothing", at that moment part of me died. After class I asked if I could talk to him, he agreed. I explained to him what I was going through he instantly apologized, but the damage was already done.

After going through so much abuse, I felt like everybody at my school knew what was happening to me. I didn't give people eye contact because my eyes told a story my mouth couldn't tell. A year later, I did what my nursing teacher said I would do, I dropped out. It was easier for me to stay home so I could monitor my mother's behavior, rather walk into an ambush. A few years later I obtained my GED and enrolled in college. My favorite subject, *Human Behavior*. This would be the weak foundation on which I began building upon, which lead me into the wilderness.

I was the black sheep of the family. The one who could never do anything right. I found myself trying to buy my family's love. As long as I had my social security checks I wasn't talked about, not that much. I felt like I was moving in slow motion. I was disliked so much that I took on other people's personalities, I didn't know who I was anymore.

October 1985. My best friend and I moved into an apartment. My best friend didn't have any money, so I paid for everything. I didn't have any money left after paying the bills, so I went on strike and refused to pay any bills. January, we were evicted. My friend moved in with her grandmother and I moved in with another friend who lived in the same building. She was the manager's sister. One day she was expecting company and wanted me to leave, but I had no place to go. She suggested that I take her brother up on his offer and go out with him. He was 37 and I was 18, to me that was like going out with my grandfather. But of course, I was at her mercy, I went. I only had twenty-five cents to my name. I took it just in case I needed to make an emergency phone call. We went to a jazz club; I was quiet the whole time. He bought me a $1.75 drink, I nursed that drink all night. After leaving the club he told me that I owed him something for the drink. I nervously told him as soon as I get some money I would pay him back the $1.75. That wasn't good enough. He drove past our exit and drove to Belle Isle Park in Detroit. Surrounded by nothing but water, he said he was going to kill me. That he had killed before and gotten away with it. We sat there for a while as he was calling me names.

Then he said because he loved his sister he wasn't going to kill me, but he was going to rape me, and he did. He drove me back to the apartment. He told me that if I told anyone he would kill me anyway, but if I did say anything no one would believe me, because I went out with him. By the time I made it to my friend's apartment I was shaking and in tears. She looked at me and said, "Please tell me he didn't do what I think he did". I asked her what she meant. She went on to tell me how he spent time in prison for throwing a woman out of a window, and how he had fondled their niece. I asked why she would suggest that I go out with him, she said she thought he had changed. I never blamed her for what her brother did, she truly wanted to believe that he had changed. A week later I told my aunt, the one whose love I had to pay for, she said, "Don't worry about it. Oh, by the way, do you have some money I saw these shoes I wanted to buy". I knew then that life wasn't worth living.

I left my friend's apartment. I went over to my best friends' mothers house, where she was staying. I had been there for a week. One day her stepfather came home early from work. She didn't want him to know that she was there, so she hid in the closet. He knocked on the bedroom door and asked where my friend was. I told him that she

had left. He proceeded to come into the room and sat down on the bed. He suggested that he would take care of me if I would be his girlfriend. I honestly couldn't believe that this was happening. My friend, still in the closet watched the whole thing. Of course, I said no, he begged then left. My friend came out of the closet, completely appalled at what she heard, stated that she was going to tell her mother. I thought to myself, thank God she witnessed what happened everything would be okay, so I thought. When her mother found out, she was angry with me instead of him. I had to leave.

The horror of life went on. February, I found out that I was pregnant, now I'm homeless and broke. I tried to get an abortion. When I had the money, I didn't have transportation, or I would have transportation and no money. I didn't know much about God, but I knew that He wanted that child here. So, I quit trying. During the pregnancy, I found myself at the mercy of complete strangers. I thought that if you were nice to people, they would be nice to you.

I learned the hard way, that wasn't true. They treated their animals better than me. Sometimes I had to sleep in abandon buildings. I didn't see a doctor until my 5th month, that's because I was hospitalized for pneumonia. After getting out of the hospital I needed a place to stay. I begged my uncle if I could stay with him. He reluctantly agreed. I stayed for a month until I was better. He sat me down and told me that I had to go, and I better be gone before he came home from work. It wasn't because I was touching things, or not cleaning up. I'm the kind of person who sits quietly in one spot. I do not touch anything unless you instruct me to. He just wanted me gone because I was pregnant. This went on until I finally went back to my mother's house. And the abuse didn't stop because I was pregnant. She would try to kick me in my stomach, but this time I fought back. This went on until I gave birth. This all happened from the age of 5 to 19. The next chapters will deal with events later in life.

Chapter 4
Betrayal

Psalm 69; 71:10-11; 109:2-5; 142
When there is abuse in your life you attract
negativity to you like a magnet.

When betrayal arrived on the scene it brought
with it much pain and sorrow. Here is where I
would experience hatred and bitterness for the
first time in my life.

Whenever I help a person its always from the
heart. I love giving and helping people, especially
friends I consider family. Nobody enters a
relationship with the idea of being the *ONLY*
person giving. No relationship such as;
husband/wife, parent/child, or a best friend
relationship will survive being one-sided. It takes
both parties involved to make it work. It's a two-
way street. But for some reason, people took my
kindness for weakness. If they were in need, I was
there best friend. The moment the tables turned,
and I was the one in need, now I'm a problem.

My mother died on June 6, 2008, I expected all
the people I was there for, to be there for me. That
wasn't the case. Two people stepped up which I

totally appreciated, but the rest completely walked away. Psalm 35:11-16, I knew exactly how David felt, I was now living it. After these individuals got back on their feet they threw me away and began posting insulting things on social media. We had people calling us picking fights for no reason. It was overwhelming. After dealing with that, I now must prepare for the funeral. The morning of my mother's funeral I had to take my child to doctor to get their test results. I was absolutely devastated at what I heard. This will be talked about in the next chapter.

Three months later, my uncle found my brother for me. At this time, I hadn't seen my brother in 28 years. When I called I was so happy to hear his voice, but I noticed he wasn't happy to hear mines. I informed him that our mother died. He said, "Oh", paused, "Oh really". He explained that he didn't care, after what she had done to him. I was still shocked by his response. I called him two more times before he told me to only call him once a year, that would be good enough for him. But he talks to other family members and childhood friends all the time. Needless to say, I never called him again. After that *TKO,* I regrouped and moved on.

November was my ordination. I had been ordained a Pastor and Prophetess. I had a few older ministers that wanted to help me in my ministry. I thought to myself this is going to be awesome. The following month, December, we started holding services at one of the minister's house. I started feeling in my spirit that there was a Judas in the midst, and I was right. One of the ministers was honest enough to tell me what this individual was planning. She planned to use me for my finances and my connections, and then dump me. It was too much for me to deal with, so I walked away from it all. All this happened within 6 months.

January, I decided to stop the ministry. I was so burned out from everything. I told God I was done with His people, but not with Him. I would later learn that you can't separate the two. You can't walk away from one without walking away from the other.

Psalm 35: 11-28 comes to mind as I write this section.

The female I was a best friend to for 15 years, in my night season, of course, she betrayed me. She went around telling people things that I had not said, or she would bring up things that had said over a decade ago, as though I had just mentioned it. But this time because of the season I was in she did a whole lot of damage. I walked into

situations with people who she had gossiped with and I was totally mistreated. What upset me the most was that they were Pastors/Leaders who should have known better. I don't know about your Bible, but mines say, if you have an ought against your brother take it to them, and Proverbs teaches you about a person who causes division.

God wouldn't let me defend myself. This is where betrayal had a baby, its name, *BITTERNESS*. Shortly after dealing with this betrayal, my children and my ex-husband started on the same path. Now, this was hard for me to deal with. My eldest son loves and craves attention. He's a very handsome young man and he loves the attention that his looks attract. He wanted to introduce me to one of his new friends. I'm the kind of mother who would welcome my children's friends and treat them like my own. As long as I didn't sense any evil in my spirit. Well, this particular day was a movie and popcorn night. Normally it's a lot of us, but this time it was only my son and his friend. The friend looked at me and said, "Your nothing like he described", I asked what he meant by that. He goes on to tell me that my son described me as some type of crack head who was never there. I turned the TV off and I'm trying not to reap my sons face off. My son starts to talk fast trying to explain that that's not what he said. His friend said no you didn't say that, but that's the picture we come up with. The friend stated that he hated me after that conversation. But after meeting me things didn't add up. Not only are you beautiful on the outside, but you're also beautiful on the inside too. I later went to a few of my son's friends and asked them if he had described me this way to them. They stated that he had, but they knew better. That went on until 2015.

My daughter, after falling in love with a joker I begged her not to get with, turned on me. This kid and his family had a horrible past. Red lights were flashing all in my spirit, but she wouldn't listen. One day we had a meeting with her and this kid. By this time, I was extremely sick in my body and we didn't know why. My ex-husband and I were pleading with her not to make this colossal mistake. She jumped up and stated that was her business, and she got this. My daughter and I have been very close up to that point, and that was very devastating to hear. It took a few months before she woke up from that nightmare.

2013, my ex-husband and I were still married at the time when he started going around lying on me. I'm the type of person who loves staying at home, so I didn't see my neighbors that often. My ex is like my son, craves attention.

A few days before Christmas, one night our neighbor was sitting in his car as we were walking in. He and my ex-started laughing and talking, he handed my ex a case of imported beers. I said, "hello", no answer I thought he may not have heard me, so I said, "hello, playing Santa Claus tonight?", he stops smiling and looked at me and said, "children stay in children place" and fist pumped my ex. Of course, my ex-stood there with complete fear on his face, because he knew he was busted. After we made it into our apartment I asked him what he had done. He knows that I hear from God, so he came with the truth. I found out that he had bad-mouthed me to every one of his family members and friends. After getting busted, he kept his mouth closed, at least until our

divorce. Not only had I dealt with his cheating, but I also had to deal with his lying too. Betrayal will cause the spirit of bitterness to overtake you and it's very hard to get rid of it.

Chapter 5
SICKNESS

The morning of my mother's funeral, June 13, 2008. I had to take one of my children to the doctors to get their test results. I was already numb from my mother's unexpected death. To add insult to injury, the doctor tells us something that would change our lives forever (for the sake of my child's privacy I will not say what it is). This diagnosis would be just the beginning of many more to come. We made it through the funeral, and life goes on. December, another one of my children started passing out on their way to school, we had no idea what was going on. I took my child to the doctor and we found out it was epilepsy. This was devastating to hear; no loving parent wants to see their children suffer from an illness.

2010-11, my health started to spiral out of control. I started having problems with my lower back. If I sat for longer than 5 minutes, I would need assistance standing up and walking. My blood sugar started spiking, but they could never catch it. Whenever I went to the doctor there would be nothing wrong. I stayed in bed for days at a time. Then I found out that I had hearing loss, so now I must wear hearing aids. This is where God begins to deal with my childhood traumas, I will talk about that in the next chapter. September 2011, I started experiencing chest pains. I later found out that my heart would stop/start on its own. After several hospital visits and a few stress test performed, they could not understand why this was happening. So, each time they sent me home and told me to deal with it. At this point, I wasn't praying or doing anything spiritual. I started questioning everything that I had ever believed in. This went on for 2 years.

By 2012, I'm forcing myself to pray. I felt that God was far away from me. There was nothing, but complete silence. My prayer life lasted like that for 2 years before I begin to feel His presence again, I couldn't give up. I was praying up to 3 hours a day. I knew it wasn't about what I felt, it was about what He created me for, *WORSHIP*.

2013, earlier I mentioned how my blood sugar would spike and they could never catch it. Well, they finally caught it. I was told if I didn't lose 10 pounds in 30 days I would have to take diabetic meds. That same year I had found out that my father's mother, sister, and niece died of diabetes, heart disease and early stages of Demetria. My cousin was only 47, this frightened me. I waited

60 days before I went back to the doctor. I went on a low carb diet and lost 25 pounds. Since then I take nothing but supplements, eat healthily and exercise.

June 2013, I had to have emergency surgery, to have my gallbladder removed.
After this, I began to pray and fast like a crazy person. I didn't understand exactly what God wanted, or what I did to deserve all of this. I felt like He HATED me!

For 6 months I would fast (2) 3 day fast a week. Yes, that's right I only ate once a week, 4 days a month. If I was going to die it would be because I was doing something spiritual, instead of allowing Satan to take me out. Things started to slowly change, *S L O W L Y*. The Holy Spirit began guiding me towards info about supplements that I would later find out I was deficient of.

I was deficient of vitamin D, (my doctor knew about this, but didn't inform me), and a few amino acids. One by one I begin to implement them into my daily life. I researched and found out that any and every illness, mental or physical has something to do with a deficiency of one or more amino acids, vitamins or minerals. Today I feel wonderful. All the glory belongs to God.

Chapter 6
Religious Mentality

Mark 7:13, Making the word of God of none effect through your tradition, which ye have delivered: and many such like things do ye.

A religious spirit is an issue that will stop the move of God in this hour we live in. Most people don't even realize they're operating under this spirit because a religious spirit has the power to make you believe that the religious things you are doing are the will of God. After researching the internet, I found a few sure signs you're operating under this spirit:

- You judge other people by their appearance
- You try to earn God's love and salvation
- You try to conform to outward holiness without inward transformation.
- You are always critical of other people's walks with God.
- Your closest Christian relationships are based only on ministry activities.
- You perform Christian duties but have no passion or hunger for God.

- You desire position and honor in the church more than honor from God.
- Your identity is rooted in a lifestyle of Christianity instead of in Christ.
- You know about the truth of Jesus but not the way of Jesus.
- You project righteousness but inwardly are filled with anger and resentment.
- You view God as a cold, harsh, distant taskmaster

When I started the dark night, this spirit was alive and active. I thought I was doing the work of God, while all along I was operating under the spirit of religion and man's traditions. You can't get closer to God with a religious mentality, this monster must be eradicated.

In my night season, the Lord revealed to me that in my heart I put Him on the level of man. I didn't trust Him. On a few occasions instead of allowing Him to help His people, I played wonder woman and tried to do it myself. In my heart, I didn't believe that He would show up on time. Gods timing is not our timing. Now listen, I was more shocked than you when I found out about all of this. It wasn't always like that, the more tests I went through the more it chipped away at my faith. And of course, my pass had a lot to do with it. I was taught how to look, act and talk Holy, but was never taught true Holiness until later in my walk. I operated in 7 out of the 11 listed above. Walking in just one of them will hinder your walk with God.

This revelation hurt me to know that I felt this way about my Heavenly Father. He showed me one by one each person I had unrighteously judged. A few of them I was able to apologize to. Then, one by one He showed me each situation where I played wonder woman. I couldn't bear the shame and the guilt that I felt. It took a long time for me to forgive myself, and of course, that's another issue of itself.

Chapter 7
Path of Forgiveness

This is something I didn't want to do because it dealt with confrontation. Confronting people who wronged me, who I had wronged or confronting myself.

Being confined to the bed, as I mentioned in the previous chapters, I kept seeing this little girl. At first, I couldn't see her face, but I was holding her hand. She was so sad and every time I saw the vision I would begin to cry. I could feel this little girl's pain, I would ask God who she was, but of course no answer. This went on for about 3 to 6 months before I found out who she was. One day the vision came in much clearer, and to my surprise it was me.

It was the age where the pain of rejection entered. As an adult I found myself being a people pleaser. I never could understand why I was like that. It wasn't with everyone, only a select few. I hated that about myself. In this vision, God showed me when and where it started. As I was holding little Ronnie's hand, I saw how she was trying to get people to be her friend. As a child, I had very thick glasses and would get teased a lot because of it. I was brown skinned on top of that, back then it was all about light skinned with long hair. I've always wanted to be accepted and loved. I could never get that from a few important people in my life. After my father's death; I was told repeatedly that he never wanted me because I was a girl. He didn't want to have anything to do with me and that my brother was his favorite. This went on for years. The Lord allowed me to feel the rejection and the pain every time my mother mentioned it. I had to forgive him for not wanting me and her for telling me. On this journey, I had to forgive everybody for the things that were done or said to me. With a few people that took a while before true forgiveness came. But after that journey, I haven't seen little me anymore.

2011, My eldest son found out that he was conceived through rape. That was something I wanted to take to my grave. But God said, not so.

When he found out I thought he would sympathize with me, but instead, he blamed me. He couldn't understand my pain. I felt like I was being raped all over again. I felt helpless. I had to remember where I was, *The Wilderness*. We all were perplexed at his response; this went on for 4 years. Dealing with this and his wild imagination made it difficult to forgive.

2015, I was at my breaking point. I had decided that I had to walk away from my own child, enough was enough. One day a family friend decided to do an intervention with him. We sat him down and questioned him, trying to understand his thinking process. I knew it was a stronghold. After much talking and tears, eventually, there was a breakthrough. Needless to say, he didn't understand why he felt the way he did. Our relationship is much better today. We're taking it one day at a time.

I found forgiving others was much easier than forgiving myself, that would take a few more years. It was hard for me to forgive myself for what I had done to God, and I also blamed myself for how other people treated me too. Somehow it had to be my fault to have all these people treat me so cruel. But after much praying and fasting forgiveness came.

January 2018. It's been 10 years, I AM OUT. I'm in recovery mode from some of the hellish events that I endured during the wilderness. This is where I lay before the Lord with fasting and praying, seeking healing for my soul from the individuals who were the closest to me. I've forgiven them, but I must be healed.

Chapter 8
Conclusion

In the wilderness, you have so many things that will happen, and it's all to break you. Your dreams, hopes, plans, ministry's, all will die. Everything about you dies. Here you are completely emptied out so that He can fill you up to overflowing with HIM. You're filled with humility and love.

You feel like you are invisible. People don't see you, nor do they hear you. I would try to have a conversation with people, and they looked at me like I had two heads. Everybody's experience is different, and some people go through it more than once. I must give a TV minister, who has gone on to be with the Lord, a great big Thank You. For being an obedient servant of God for teaching this to the world. Before then I never knew there was another name for it.

I thank God that it happened. It has made me a much stronger person. I can finally say that I love myself. I embrace my weirdness and everything about me. I've also retired my wonder woman cape too. My life is solely for Him; I no longer live my life for people. I look at life and people differently. With more love and compassion.

***The reunion I've prayed and longed to happen with my brother will never happen. November 2016, my brother passed away. I will never get the opportunity to know why he excluded me from his life for 37 years. My daughter told me that God shielded me from what my brother held in his heart for me. She said God knew I wouldn't be able to take it. After she said that, my soul was at peace.

NOTES

www.ingramcontent.com/pod-product-compliance
Lightning Source LLC
Chambersburg PA
CBHW021121020426
42331CB00004B/569

9 780359 697786